Smuggling Cherokee

Smuggling Cherokee

Kim Shuck

The Greenfield Review Press
Greenfield Center, New York

Published by The Greenfield Review Press, P.O. Box 308, Greenfield
Center, New York 12833

ISBN 0-87886-146-7
Library of Congress Number: available on file

Permissions are listed on page 71.

Cover and interior design by Sans Serif, Inc., Saline, MI
Printed in the United States

For My Family
I love you all
For the moments when you were supportive
And the ones when you were not
Gran, Dad, Mom, Dave, Eddie, Briall, Morgan, Brian,
Greg, Mary Jean, Ruth, Kate, Carol Lee, Stephanie, Allison,
Denny, Thelma, Karl, Mike, Sebastian, Kelly
Most recently Christine and Danielle
First last and always for my Great Grandma
Etta Mae Rowe

April Morning
Prayer to the East

The smell of that spring flooded pecan grove clings to us yet.
Through that old book mustiness
Academia,
Through recycled airport
And hotel room
Loneliness.

This woman's soul
Has come to rest at the edge of your body
Let it linger there.

Hold me and just let me be
That small town Indian woman.
Symbol of nothing in particular.
And you can be
That Indian man.
Whatever other shapes we choose to wear
Singularly or in
Groups
Let them stay in the suitcases.

Water as a Sense of Place

1.
The water I used to drink spent time
Inside a pitched basket
It adopted the internal shape
Took on the taste of pine
And changed me forever.

I remember
Carrying that basket from the pump,
The slow swell of the damp roots,
Sway of a walk
That made carrying it easier.

Sometimes I imagine Step's Ford,
Both in and out of flood,
Tar Creek
Spring River
In and out of baskets.

Gram's hands
Long, smooth fingers powerful and exact
Pull and twist
Sorting spokes and splitting weavers
Constructing my idea of water.

2.
I forgot to ask for the name
Of the creek that used to run through
What is now my backyard.

They piped it under,
But with enough rain
It remembers where to go.

Returns to shift
Mud and
Retaining walls.

It is, I imagine,
Referred to somewhere downtown
By the number of its pipe.

3.
Early training holds fast.
I sleep with water to the East of me,
Wake humming or singing
And go to water.

Bareheaded
In all but the most violent rainstorms
A connection I cannot give up
My hair and lashes glittering at first then weighed down.

I throw my windows open to the rain and
Lean out into the shock of contact.
Water so thick in the air
All but my closest neighbors are erased.

Rain is not an emergency
Not in October
Not in this place
I take it in breath by breath.

Because The Feet of Four Indian Women Might Change the Weather on the East Coast

Dancing on this slightly uneven ground,
We circle with the fire always on our right.
Our feet are the accurate feet
Of southern style traditional dancers.
We place them very carefully
Each time we take
Small steps
To the music.

We are pink and blue and green and dark brown.
Our hair is braided
And decorated
According to individual equations.
Nothing is left to chance.

We are connected by the
Drum.
The fringes on our shawls shift
In exact patterns
They describe the movement
Of turbulent water or
The stars.

Our feet hold a message too.
They say:
We are proud
Proud
Proud
Proud of you.

Some Things I Know About Love that Might be of Some Use

1.
I cannot take a handful of dirt from my backyard without seeing a
      woman.
She has a crooked left eyetooth, solid hips and thighs
And hair that reaches to her knees.
When she tips her head back she can feel her hair
Caressing her calves, the small of her back.
I can see her gathering cress here
Some four hundred years ago.

I have to wonder with each handful of dirt
What part of this dirt contains her hair?

As I plant my squash
I am grateful
That she cares for me in this way.

2.
I have heard the old women say
That the children look like the parent
Who had the most fun making them.

I wonder at the curl in my hair
And my grandmother's story of the escaped slave
Taken in
And loved so intensely
By her great-grandmother
That the erotic aftershock

Curls the hair of one member of the family
Per generation
Ever since.

3.
Sometimes I see a flash of gold/brown light
In someone's eye.
And I smell the flooded pecan grove
Near grandma's house.
I wonder if this is what it is for salmon
Swimming upstream.
Some small taste of the familiar
That sets their sense of direction.

And I think about my father
With a shiver for the bravery
Of trusting someone else's sense of direction.

4.
Some things are more important than the time they take.

5.
This scrubby grey mint
Was snatched from death
On a hot day near Petaluma.
It rode in a wet tissue
All the way to San Francisco.
And despite only having had
Half an inch of root
It flourishes.

Lecturing in Indian Studies on the Eve of the Millennium

Floored by the student's question,
I try to see myself through His eyes
But cannot get past the woman in the mirror.
Scarred lip and eyebrow
Remnant, overly casual
Stance and drawl of an
Ex bar fighter.
I clear my throat,
"I can tell you
How to get good at nine ball,
What bars in North Eastern Oklahoma
Offer you a glass with your beer,
Or I could talk about weaving, today's lecture topic.
But if you want Indian wisdom
About peace
You should avoid asking those
With scars on their knuckles."

Home Songs

1.
Always consider the possibility that you take yourself too seriously.

2.
That dry cleaners is built
On the most sacred spot
In four counties.

It was not intended as an act of irreverence.
They didn't ask and we
Were too embarrassed for them
To say.

Yeah, sometimes I get angry.
Most often when
I can't find any dirty laundry
So I can go pray.

3.
Just 'cause you don't know the stories,
Doesn't mean there aren't any.

4.
It's been ten years since I was home, but
Jake doesn't even look up from the paper
As I enter his store.
"Your Gram is out of flour.
You want tea you have to buy it.
Milk's probably soured."

I love you too old man.

5.
Humor and food are the trickiest
Of cultural artifacts,
But overlaps do occur.

My Polish and Tsalagi relatives
Sat down one evening and enjoyed
Potato pancakes together.

And then there was the afternoon
Of near delirium:
28 Elderly Indians
Listening to Seuss in translation.

Packrat

There is a danger in words
Spoken with intent.

Twelve years of
Ribbons off chocolate boxes
Little papers
Written with one or two words
And dried seed pods.
Preserving a sense of romance
A promise of generative power
A trust in my own skill
In directed strength.
I think,
"Who is this woman?"
And pull something out of the box:
A bit of red velvet ribbon.
But I never could read for myself.

These agreements we make:
Blue is what we call this or that vibration
Scales up to purple
No way of knowing if you see it
The same way that I do.

What is intuition anyway?
Knowing
Water resonating in the stem of a tomato plant
Robins in the candleberry getting drunk.

I braid a wish into my hair
Take a breath
And sit down to write.

Fossil

What happened that
Our measuring tools have
Become too sensitive
To be useful?
Reflect a passion for
Measuring
More than one
For understanding.

I operate so often on instinct,
Headlong unconsidered impulses
Backed by hints of
Important scraps of
Information.

And I don't know what it is
To be sure of anything.
When we look at the little pieces
We can see how fast
Or where
They go
But not both at the same time.
Certainty is so fugitive a thing
And whether years or bad choices
Wear it down
Water and human nature are so patient that
Confidence is gradually replaced by
Practice.

In a Time of Smoke

1
Stand still and light a fire
All around me,
Watch it spread and
Trust in what I think I know about fire.

It burns hot and fast
Takes out the understory.
I listen to the smell of burning panic grass
And feel my hair lifted and twisted into witch's knots.

2
In a time of smoke
The smoke, smoke might be the message.

3
Grass fires burn fast and hot
But not very deep.
If you can overcome
The fear that the flammable have of fire
You can walk through
More or less
Untouched.

4
Smoke from a scavenger fire
Flame wind twists erratic at the crest of the hill
Reveals a seam of rock
But it can't take out a tree.

The wind runs hard before the flames
Knots the smoke.
Grass and dead branches
But nothing living taken.

5
I place a candle in an East facing window
In memory or calling of some unknown thing.
It frets and itches in
The cold that leaks through the glass.

Predictions

For Eric

Some tell the future by
Looking at the roots of plants,
The thickness of a squirrel's fur.
We all have our own calendars.

I am arrested from
Time to time by the things
Happening outside of my circle of effort:
Rain water trapped in the hollow of a rock,
Butterfly and salmon migrations.
Sometimes my expectation of an emergency
Blurs my awareness.
Sometimes my awareness blurs everything else.

Saturn rose tonight
Over the tree that the ravens live in,
Later the moon
Winter rich in the sky.

I watch the hawk
Battle in an unfamiliar wind,
Necessity creating grace.
See a plane
Above him
And wonder if you might be on that plane.
I worry for you when you can't put
Your feet on the ground for more than a few days at a time.

The honeysuckle grew well this year
I will weave you a basket
And no matter what you put in it
All you can take out are images of home.

Winter 2001

The Overseers of Complexity

1.

I have an innate fascination for gadgetry
Old constructions of brass and glass and numbers
Designed to measure one thing or another.
Enjoy compasses and sextants
Things with gears
Or wires that spin
Something meant to determine location.
The ritual adjustment of the divining tool appeals.
If I can just get the alignment
When the proper stars are up
And present the correct offerings to the overseers of complexity
Perhaps I will know where I am.

I like small brown rocks for the same reason.

2.

Fits of homesickness come and go,
Obeying no known rules of logic.
I may be getting off a plane from Oklahoma
And already be missing the heavy, wet air
Smell of terrapin
Mine tailings
The flood plain of the Neosho river.

3.
Stirring the creek water,
"A-m (a')",
She said.

Later I asked her,
"Is it still
Water
When it comes out of the tap?"

4.
While planting the garden
I discover
Four mason jars containing
Words on paper.
Pages torn from a
Ledger book,
Covered in
Tiny writing.
Three seem to be poems
One just says:
"Beans".

A Basket Defines A Space

1
I watch the sparrows fluff
Loose dirt into their
Feathers.
Then
Place the palms of my hands
Precisely
In the hollows left
By their small bodies.

I bruise the geranium leaves
Both
To smell the pepper/ apricot/ lemon rose smells
And to feel their textures
Stiff and rough as old lace
Or smooth as sueded silk.

I know that I have never been touched
By another person
The way that I touch these things,
With knowledge and reverence
With clarity.

2
All of the good stories change from one telling
To the next.
But in my life there are a few that stubbornly
Refuse.

There is a mass grave under the playground
A block and a half from where I weave.
When the rains come heavy
In some years
Calcium deposits appear
On the sidewalk.

3
"To make a work basket,
You need to know the shape of your work,"
That old lady said.

Grandmother,
I don't know whether to thank you
Or to cry.

Family Story

One version of the story goes like this:

Having been abandoned by her husband
My very young cousin
Waits with a shotgun
Until she hears her mother's car
Coming to a stop in front of the house.
When she is sure that her mom
Will always wonder
If the car could have been parked a little quicker,
She pulls the trigger.

About 1500 miles away I fall to the floor of my room
Nose gushing blood like
No barfight with hick border-billies
Ever made it do.
Incoherent for hours
Brother applying cold rags to the back
Of my neck
I become alert just in time
For the phone call.

There was a note.

It took chemicals and an expert to remove enough
Blood and brain matter
For it to be readable.

The note explained nothing.

Her older sister insisted on
Being the one to clean the room.
We have never spoken about this
But I can clearly see her in my dreams
Scrubbing walls
Scrubbing
Scrubbing.
Trying to make the room livable.

This is one version of the story.
It fails to explain why her husband had her
Wedding rings.
And hocked them
The week of her burial.

I am told by elders,
By tradition
By experience
That I had one year to mourn this.
That the statute of limitations on grief
In our community does not allow
The self-indulgence
Of carrying this on for longer than it took
For my hair to grow back.
At the end of the year I sang
Friends brushed and braided my
Squeaky
New washed hair
And I reclaimed my life.

I carry with me stories
Oddly enough
The one that I remember most often
Is an argument we had
As small children.
This memory isn't kind to either of us,
But when the fight ended
We curled up with crayons
And coloring books.
I made the roses on my page
"Indian Red"

Sometimes

Sometimes I can
Hold in my mind
The perfect vision of what
Weeds can become.
The structure
Curves
Absolute as eggshell.

That weekend
A cloud of hummingbirds
Moved into my backyard.
It's too little to say that
Things have changed.
How could I ever
Become used to
Clouds of hummingbirds?
Designed to be noticed,
The males show off
In steep parabolas.

Do you see
That the arc that took you
There
Reflects the one
That brought me here?
It's no accident that
Process favors
Symmetry.

Sometimes I can
Hold an image of writing
The very last poem I need.
And with
Nothing more to investigate.
I fall asleep
Curled against you.

The Collection of Known Things

1.
In this dream I navigate by touch
Brush walls and add
To the collection of known things.
Loose my connection going through a
Doorway
And never find it again.
It's always a toss
Whether I
Stand still
Or keep
Walking.

2.
Somewhere in my imagination
There is the gleam
Of use polished brass.
Tools handled into beauty
Some kind of equation there
Use-need-grace
A form of comfort I think.

3.
It's got to be a sort of discipline
Being willing to
Use your senses
Learn publicly.
Being willing to worry people.
It's an ongoing project
Managing the collection of known things.

4.
Paradox is a constant.
The gleam of use polished brass.
Have to keep remembering
The responsibility of caretaking information
Does not outweigh
The responsibility to transform mistakes
Into good choices.

Breathing

Two am and
The windchange pulled me out of sleep.
I was thinking of you
But didn't know it yet.
Thought the cold was an issue of
An open window
One too few blankets
Need for a cup of tea.
Stood at the window and thought about
Sleeping neighbors.

For at least a year now
I've held you
With careful hands,
Tracked you through your days
Gently.

Two weeks later
Rain pulls me out of sleep
Find myself twined around
Your jacket.
The plausible tactile memory-
Your mouth very slightly on mine-
Shudders through me and
I cannot get back to sleep.
Go into my garden
Fill my hands with wet rosemary.

I take a relative measure
The number of palm widths
Across your shoulders.
Try to remember careful hands
Careful.

You play in trapezoidal prisms
Step six more inches into the light
Breathe for both of us. A hum,
I can feel it in the palms of my hands
The back of my neck
Arch of my left foot
And the back of my jaw.
If there are words I can't hear them.
I'll sit in the back right corner
Just out of the light, where I will be warm.

Crows Watching Out for Me

There is the rustle and catch
Of leaves, dry and falling
Of crows teasing flight.
As always I am distracted
By the details.

Green Eyes is in the corner remaking tobacco.
That part is important.
I need to remember that he's there.

It rained the other day.
The lemon thyme is making
A comeback.
When there's enough
I'll bake bread.

I hear his voice in a language so sharp it makes me weak.
He speaks to the seven fires, to the red panther.
I could be in trouble here.

I look up from my digging to
The San Francisco skyline
Lighting up for evening.
I struggle with life algorithms.
Trees still throw more weight of water in a day
Than people do of steel and concrete.

Green Eyes fires something with a safety match.
I hear him do it, smell sage and wild tobacco.
An ache begins in the center of me,
The crows release me with a sound.

It's time to trim the grape.
Sap has fallen and
There are round, orange
Warm afternoons
And cinnamon.
In two weeks there will be pine tea.
A short attention span might just save my life.

The Logic Within the Relationship

At 8:30
The largest dragonfly I'd
Ever seen
Crashed into my window.
6 1/2 inches tip to tip
She was stunned and
Fell two stories to the grass.
Who knows what she was seeing
That made my window
Such an urgent target?

The logic within the relationship
Person to person
Person to object
Space to thing
Doesn't have to hold up
Anywhere else.

I live in a place
Where water
Hangs so often
Heavy in the air
That I can taste ocean salt
On everything,
Ripe peaches, your shoulder.

Hard to remember that
Water is so rare in some places.
When you need to hunt it
Any reflective surface
Glass
Glossy paint
Or even
A sheet of ice
Can look promising.

These stories get told over and over.
I close my eyes and
Tell them to myself.
I think that shiny surface is water
Say a short prayer
Not recognizing the blue grey car hood.

Four years
Showering in a cedar paneled
Room.
Now cedar smells like wet to me.
Some mornings find me
Singing to trees.
Old songs
Wrong coast
And bark patterns like
River eddies.
I might expect to pull
Rainbow trout from
The margin of the wood.

The logic within the relationship
Can and does
Lead us all to
Fits of silliness
Dramatic mistakes
Common mishaps.
People need to know each other
As viewed and viewer.
It's magical thinking
Smoke and flame
A pane of ice as
Mirror.

Smuggling Cherokee

1.
I unroll my map
And a photocopy
Of the palm of my left hand,
Weigh down the corners with
A fist sized chunk of peach colored flint, a
Barite rose
Some gypsum and
A piece of ruby jack
Then set in to work.

2.
There is a certain art
To a good mistranslation.

3.
I remember the rage and impatient violence.
These days
I'm more likely
To pile river rocks in the bathtub
For love of smooth things.
Things as edgeless as I can make them.

4.
The man asks me,
  "Do you speak Cherokee?"
But it's all I ever speak,
The end goal of several generations of a
smuggling project.
We've slipped the barriers,
Evaded border guards.
I smile,
"Always".

The Dream of Being a Larger Mammal

I don't remember seeing a pair of blue eyes
Till I was in my teens.
And I don't ever remember a smile like this one.
I want to relax into his confidence.
Let this man guard my sleep.
We both know we'll be in different cities tomorrow.
And I know I will break my heart over this.

I have the dream again.
The one about swimming with
Large unseen
Warm-blooded
Animals
Under green water.
I forget what it means
But it has to be important
I have it so often.
Something brushes my leg
And I wake up.

I comb smoke through my hair,
Put on that old red shirt
That he left
And sing softly to myself.
For so long my energy thrown
Into a very old war
Not over yet.
I know what goes into building proteins

Or large buildings
But what trace minerals do I need to remake trust?

In my dream
I'm wearing a nightgown
As I swim it pulls and billows against my thighs.
My hair is dragged back by the water.
Need something,
Want
Contact?
And I wake up.

I always wanted to be
A more elegant beast.
Lovers, friends describe me
A hamster pushing nesting material
Or
An otter cracking seashells.
A woman of quick and purposeful activity.
A small woman
Soft fur and action
With tiny clever hands.

We're going to the beach
I'm barefoot
Wear a skirt and an old red shirt
The shirt isn't buttoned.
I'm hot and cold
My head is in his lap
We're driving too fast.
The images crack in my mind
Ice or
Lollipops
And as his hand drops to my hair
I wake up.

Downpour

In a sharp and gentle moment
I am promised rain
For the holidays,
And later while Morgan sits
Intently painting
Chocolate butterflies—
Rivers full
Baskets full
Hands full
Mouths full
Of rain
Pound the windows.
Suddenly I remember to laugh.

I wake in tossed covers
Vague touches
Dreams of walking in wet grass
Barefoot
Smiling.
Walk into the morning red
With a song
I'm thinking something
Learning something here.

Briall is tying knots in string
I wonder what she is saving
But she's so focused
I don't want to distract her.
These children that I somehow set in motion

Growing and becoming mysterious.
Purple and black knots
Line up on her string.

I consider burning something
Don't know what yet.
Feel greedy for symbols
But some things won't become
Symbolic
Even when I was promised rain.

I watch my hand
Sneak out a window into the water.
Eddie is folding stars
From something that glitters.
Morgan outlines the edge of a wing
Curved brow of red
Then paints
Eyespots.
Briall ties another knot.
And I look at my winter gift
A handful
A mouthful
Of rainwater.

Winter 2002

The Needs of Scientific Research
Must be Respected

1.
Shopping for my son's birthday present I find
Microscopes
At a store I have patronized for a while.
In large letters on the box "Free piece of Peruvian mummy wrap
    inside."
Mummy wrap
Used to wrap
A dead
Body.

Mummy wrap.

2.
To my knowledge most cultures have taboos about playing with
bits of the dead. Around the world people believe, with few
exceptions, that there is something a bit unnatural about grave
robbing. I personally find it outré to consider giving my seven-year-
old grave goods to examine. Find the cheerful lettering that
promises "scientific" access, chilling. The scrap of fabric is stiff with
either body fluids or embalming fluids, stiff with its purpose as a
final shroud for someone's loved one.

3.
In this moment I am every body from every raided grave.

I am an Egyptian lady
Used as train fuel
Or ground up
Into
Laudanum
As a medicinal
In 1902.

I am Tolund man
Pulled out of my bog
And because
The museum doesn't have space
To house my entire body,
They cut my head off and
Display it by itself.
People walk by
"How lifelike,"
They say.

I am the unnatural number
Of finger bones
Supposedly from the corpse of
John the Baptist
On display in Florence.

I am dismantled.
I am out of context.
I am abstracted.
I am contested.

I am Geronimo's skull in a glass-topped case
In a Frat house at Yale.

And while we are at it
I am probably the
Finger
Or Ear
Or breast
Severed from a dead enemy in some war.

I am proof of someone's bravery.
I am proof of someone's theory.
I am proof and I cannot be returned.

4.
How many mummies does it take
To supply fragments
For a run to toy microscopes?

If they knew it
Would the manufacturers
Tell you her name?

"Your fragment of mummy wrap
Was torn from the palm area
Of a woman named Anna.
She used to bathe her children with that hand
Caress her husband
Prepare food.
See the workbook page
To determine what bacterial activity
Created the pattern on the fabric."

The salesperson approaches
Sees me eyeing the microscopes,
"Pretty cool hunh?"
He asks.

Friday Night Show

You play those old songs
With an accent
Made up of
Concrete
Building windows reflecting
The windows and bent lines
Of other buildings and
Foggy summer mornings.
You take them places
Lives and
Landscapes they
Never rang through before.
Those Lakota words
Sing between high rises
Along nighttime streets
Far from deserted.
You sing about
Old battles
Dancing
The little and large issues of
Pow Wow,
At the same time say
'We are this also
This city
This awkward
Unaccounted for thing.
We are this deferred history.'

Ignore or notice
Approve or not
History deferred
History delayed
Happens anyway.

You eat pancakes at a diner
Between shows
Smoke a camel
Talk to the drum.
Some kind of step between
Traditional
And jazz musician.
The second set is even
Better.
On the way home
We walk past bars
Restaurants
Along nighttime streets
Far from deserted.
We talk about
Old friends
Singing
The little and large issues of
Living in this place.
Find different words for
Family
Commitment
Song.
Sometimes history delayed
Just gives us time to reflect.

Ta Lu Tsi

For Julia Parker

Someone needs to translate for the roots.
Bring stories
From last years burned
Grass.
Negotiate between
This bark
That stick.

At this time of year
The ground
Is warmer than the wind.
Stay low in a
Fold
Of faulted earth.

They may talk about this
Art
As a patience
That no one else could
Understand.
For myself it is
A panicked
Desire to see
Becoming in my
Hands.

You want your ash straight
So the best tree

Will be tight in a group of other trees.
They have to fight each other for light
So they grow straight up.
Taking the one
Will help the others grow.

Often I don't even
Look
At the whole basket
While I weave.
The pattern is just there
Unfolding for me.
I try to hold
The purpose
The identity of the
Piece
In my heart.

The best day to strip
Hickory
Will be the hottest one of the year,
Sometime mid-August
In my part of the country.
You have to sing
Leave a gift for the tree
Then mark the area
You want to take
With your knife
Before pulling it off.
Never strip
A ring around the whole thing
Or you'll kill it.
If you picked the right day
And the tree likes your song
The bark will come off in one piece.

Sometimes my urgency to
Weave
Is so intense
That I hardly breathe
Until
The last
Crossing
Is made
And the
Basket
Is
Complete.

Approaching Language as a Group Art Project

These past months
We're passing words from hand to hand.
Packets
Tins
Childproof containers full.
Remedies for headaches-
Moistly laying end to end
Drawing bruises
Over lacerations to prevent
Infection.

We fumble with
DEPRESSION
Can barely open the bottle.
It is narcotic
But then, there are no children here now.

We build collections of
HOME and
SAFE
Portion them out.
We will smuggle them
Onto airplanes.
Pass them under tongues
During visiting hours.
Whisper them into the spaces
Between songs.

We are ticketed for
Chalking them on the sidewalk.

A man in Nigeria is hanged
For distributing FAIR
Carved into bars of soap.

A woman in Utah is beaten to death
With
SILENCE.

A little girl in San Francisco drowns in
LUNG.

A traditional dancer in DC
Falls dead
HONORABLE
Beaded on his bustle.

We are in a dangerous business here.

You be careful,
Go careful.
You are making us
Fearless.
And we are teaching each other to see.

March 2003

1.
The storm's edge thins to nothing over the bay.
Caught by water temperature—
New winds
Lack of interest.

What could a map be anyhow?
Catalog of rivers, trees, and silted throughways
Or a list of instructions
From there
To
There.
Navigation can require so many senses at once,
I'm easily amazed when I get anywhere through intention.

All around the world children are throwing rocks.
I slip two pebbles into my mouth
And consider my options.

2.
In green light I watch the centuries burn.
How expensive fear can be.
There is talk of precision
As they torch the schools
The teachers
The students.
There is talk of standing together

And we are all more isolate.
The bus can't get through.
There is talk of inconvenience.

Four men are stopped on the bridge,
Arrested,
Held without phone call
They are questioned.
One had a fish.
The fish is confiscated.

3.
I wake this morning in
Fog and rain
Remember my pebbles and
Spit them
Into my hand.
What window would I put a pebble through?
I've always liked expanses of glass.
One rock is transparent,
A trapezoid
The other
A flattish oval
And brown.
So which rock do I throw,
The healing stone
Or the one
That can tell the future?

The Roots of This

The roots of this are in Connecticut—
I'm sure they are.
There or in Europe.
Your mother hunted down
Across fields in Poland.
What stories haunted your childhood?
Taught you that
If you were only perfect enough
It would pay for the new life here
Pay back the theft of this place?
So you exchange fear of soldiers
For fear of guilt.

Hail then, the history deferred.

An image from your childhood:
Children from the local reservation.
You remember them dirty and underfed . . .
And you always put in change
When they passed cans
Money to save the Indians.

Save the Indians,
Collect the whole set.

Words from our languages
Feel right in your mouth.
Only a few of the ones you know
Seem exotic anymore.

Tuxedo, ya know, wasn't always
A prom night affair.

Man on the plane from New York
From your home town, Grandma
Mouth full of beans and corn
At dinner.
Wants to talk about The Bell Curve
Wants to talk about how comforting it is
That we aren't all dead.
Then tells me that my comments about
The DHEW sterilization policies are not
Dinner conversation.
They are uncomfortable to hear about,
He says.
Oh yes, I empathize,
A little uncomfortable to live through as well.

Your guilt is not useful to me.
I love you in ways that confuse me.
Your guilt is not useful.

So I—mixed race urban Indian
Sidewalk Indian
But also
The granddaughter of Polish
Survivors of the Great Depression.
Given Chopin and other Eastern Europeans
Every Wednesday afternoon for years
At that carved
Upright
Piano
That was never really
In tune.
Dragged around to neighbor's houses

Most paid me to play
Waltz of the Flowers
Two dollars the going rate for
15 minutes of pecking at the family alter.
Eye level with the portraits of four generations
Carefully arranged on starched white crochet.
Predictable if I say I hated it
That it was an imposition on my creative spirit.
But I never thought of the piano
As an instrument for music making.
It was a teletype
A code machine
I played material connections
Code,
Not music.
I didn't hate it
I didn't love it either.
I became a very good technician,
Music was deferred for later.

I envy you,
You told me
Over and over
I always wanted to be Indian.
But we never really worked out what that meant to you.
I always wished I was as beautiful as you were
Grandma.
Always something to resent each other for.

I sit at the dining room table.
It's covered with a plastic 'cloth'
To preserve it
Protect it
Reserve it for some future date when we will
Break out the handmade lace cloth

And the good china.
A secret—
I'm drinking tea from the good china now.
Didn't you trade in labels for it
In the 40s?
Genuine bone china from England
You told me again and again
Having tea and toast
With the strawberry jam we made together last May.

Your guilt does me no good.

I wish I could have found a way to ask
Please don't fixate on the few words that still feel exotic
In your mouth.
When I make music
I do it in a language you don't speak.
I'm sorry that that seemed like such a distance
Between us.
But I'm having tea at your table now.
You gave me just as much of you
As the other side of the family did of them.
Everything so blue-collarly preserved for future want.
Including that fear the family brought from Poland.
Fear of the soldiers
Turned to fear of being the soldiers.
Fear of a need for soldiers
On the middle shelf
In the china closet.

Location Stories

1.
Living in the world of the half translated,
I catch about every other word,
Probably make
Undeserved connections
Between ideas,
And
Am
More often than not
Confused.

2.
My face
Is shaped by a language
You never knew existed.
We will call this exotic.
There is a thickness of muscle
Along my jaw
That often seems aggressive.
I notice all the wrong things.

3.
I spend the day herding
Books
Back onto their shelves,
Doing piles of laundry,
And repotting plants.
Tie spells of protection into
My children's

Shoelaces and
Send them off to school.

4.
I read portents
Into random events.
Foreshadowings of things that
I long for or
Fear.
Become exhausted by my days
In a place that is, but should not be, mine.
The location stories are too new for me
Here.
Nor am I at home in my people's
Smokey Mountains
Though I know many,
Well practiced stories
From there.

Giveaway

In gratitude for all of it- theft, small pox, relocation and denial. Wi-do.

We need to be stubborn for this work
Stubborn and loving.
The most difficult of lessons for me
Sometimes.
Generous gifts
Are often given
By those who didn't intend to give anything at all.

I call the slave master
Who lost track of my ancestor
A blanket for you
In gratitude.

I call the soldier
With a tired arm
Who didn't cut deeply enough
Into my great-great grandfather's chest to kill clean.
I return your axehead
Oiled and sharpened
Wield it against others with equal skill.

Will the boarding school officer come up?
The one who didn't take my Gram
Because of her crippled leg.
No use as a servant- such a shame with that face . . .

Finally the shopkeeper's wife
Who traded spoiled cans of fruit
For baskets that took a year each to make
Thank you, Faith, for not poisoning
Quite all
Of my
Family.

Blankets for each of you,
And let no one say
That I am not
Grateful for your care.

In the Year of the Wood Monkey

1.
I have taken the offered moment
For memory.

Draw breath and bid the rivers rise,
That language could be this too
This naming
Conjuring.

And as we slip away from one another
How do we abbreviate this?
What folds do we put in the memory
So that it will fit in the shoebox under the bed
In margins of the books we shared
On every table and bench
Of our favorite café?
I don't pretend to be good at this anymore
I think that I used to be.

Fog consumes the city
Gulp by gulp.
Aggressive in the afternoon
It grapples with everything west of Divisidero.

2.
Once upon a time I was subtle.
In Medford I pulled a shirt out of my suitcase,
Not worn in three months.
Find your hair on it

Shorter and curlier than mine.
And how does such a small thing bring me to tears?

The rain is just this side of ice
Listening to the TV news
Rain hitting the pool
Coffee perking, while getting dressed.

As we drive into Ashland
Through the cold mist
We
Pass the graveyard.
Grief
Made part of the daily landscape,
As though it were an inoculation
Small doses that make you immune
To the disease.
I brace myself for the prick of the
Tine.

It must be raining in the hills
The rivers are
In fact
Rising.

3.
New York in January
13 degrees and
Snow walked into ice
Outside the bookstore.

Your idol used to play basketball
In the park across the street.
I sit near the court and drink
Hot cocoa

So thick it tastes bloody.
Next week I'll be back in front of a classroom.

I'm like a kid in the snow
Not sophisticated at all.
Want to frolic until
Remembered sadness shakes me down.

4.
In Albuquerque they feed me
Thai food.
I can smell a fountain
And the lawn nearby.
Speak to the kids about
The memory that circles have
Of squares.

My hotel is next to a sushi parlor
In case my San Francisco self
Needs to eat sushi
In the high desert.
My rez-rat radar
Finds a diner instead
That will serve me
Green chili on pancakes for breakfast.
Afterwards I have toast and strawberry jam.

The river isn't rising here,
But the Bosque isn't on fire either.
Hotel rooms are often disorienting.
I loose east and
Fall asleep with the TV on.

There is a certain kind of woman
Who will always dream of water.

Wake to the shift of ice in the glass.
What is Johnny Depp doing on TV at 4 am?
As my plane takes off the rain starts.

5.
It has rained on me in six states this year so far
But now it's
So hot
We just get thunder in the hills.

A twelve-hour drive to get here
It'll be at least that to get back.
We sit by the golf course and talk.

Ginger tea and cigarettes
Wild weather and aggravation.
We talk about plunder and the politics of colonization.
The bodies of our dead belong to someone else,
And we are accused of superstition and over symbolism.
Later by the vending machines I contemplate
The symbolism of money itself
And the heads of the dead
Pictured there.

6.
On the morning my son turned 14
And it's almost 9 months after the fact.
Eddie and I go to Grace Cathedral to walk the labyrinth.
We light candles for Tim and Martha
One for the coming year.
Let us have learned something.
The rest of the day is friends and strawberries,
Fossils, confetti, watermelon
The party isn't always gentle with us.

Chocolate isn't gentle either
I am ravaged the morning after.
By a whole piece of chocolate cake.
I can count the remaining months on my frosting sticky fingers.

7.
The year of the wood monkey
There may be great intellectual exchange,
In monkey years
There is also the potential for
Environmental upheaval.

I take the offered moment
For memory,
Step into the wind and
Let it go.

A Prayer for Unselfish Action

I don't need to be
Right
All the time
See how I prove it.
Hah!

I curl against you
In sheets that I will not change.
Rented beds in one place or
Another.
I know that if I ever had you in
My own bed, my
Home place,
That everything would change
Between us.
It is a formality we avoid.

Those stories
Are not supposed to tell you
The correct way to do things.
They merely indicate the
Easiest way.

The memory of your hands on me
In my hair
However persuasive
Erotic
Enveloping
Is not your touch.

Guide me in these actions.
Help me to good judgment.
Let me be more kindness
Than hurt.
Place my hands carefully,
Carefully.

Contributing to the Book

'We have selected your work
For possible publication.
Please send us a photo
And a short bio'

I choose a photo
In which I appear to have
Brushed my hair.
I am staring at the camera.
I do not look like me
To me.
That should be perfect.

A 40 to 80-word biography
Is a joke.

Kim Shuck is terrified of success.
She will avoid writing this bio
For as long as possible.
She has chosen a list of
The most uncharacteristic
Things that she's ever done
To represent her in your book.

No mention is made of doing laundry.
I do not talk about the hour spent
At the supermarket yesterday
Selecting a mildew retardant
For the wall behind my largest bookshelf.

On the subject of bookshelves . . .
I do not mention the absurd number of books
That cohabit with me.
That two of my three children are named
From embarrassingly nerdy volumes that I was reading while pregnant
Or that I have invariably chosen
Partners based on their reading voices.

Instead of saying any of this I wave a shiny detail or three
The one-day workshop given for a summer program
In New Mexico,
The reading with a famous Native writer that
I agreed to do
So I could get out of town for a few days,
Or,
My membership on a board of directors that takes up
At most three hours of my time every
Few months.

By the time I am completely unrecognizable to myself
I am willing to send the requested information

The following is a list of poems that have appeared previously in other publications:

"Because the Feet of Four Indian Women Might Change the Weather on the East Coast," "Some Things I Know About Love that May Be of Some Use," and "Home Songs" were originally published in *Gatherings XI* (Theytus Books Ltd., 2000)

"Water as a Sense of Place" was originally published in Native Realities (website of the Wordcraft Circle of Native Writers and Storytellers)

"The Overseers of Complexity" and "Smuggling Cherokee" were originally published in *The Cream City Review* (University of Wisconsin 2003)

"March 2003" was published on the San Francisco Public Library website in April of 2004 as part of a series managed by the San Francisco poem Laureate devorah major

"In a Time of Smoke" (*Shenandoah 54/3*)

The following are poems that have been accepted for publications that have not come out yet.

"The Roots of This" will be coming out in a book on working class *Native Urban Folk* edited by Allison Hedge Coke

"Teaching Indian Studies on the Eve of the Millennium" will be published in a book on Indian Women Surviving Violence